"I existed in a womb, just like an abyss
Came straight from spirit land, my hands balled in a fist
Punching on my mom's stomach, kicking on her cervix
Twitching cause I'm nervous, Thought my intended purpose
Was to be born to reign, not in scorn or vain
But to take on a name, my pops chose for me…"
Nas - Fetus

Chicago via Ghana. Busses and boats. Planes and trains. The lineage of the middle passage mixed with modern migration. I am the son of migrants who came to the United States because of promises shown to them in brochures. Their vision of America was shaped by Hollywood. Cinema and sitcoms gave the impression of a life less laborious and without limits. They longed to live in that abundance. They dreamed beyond the shores of their homeland. Their hearts brimming with a love for the future they believed in for themselves and for my sister and me. Their heads filled with fears and wonders of a new world with new languages, foods, and faces. Ghana was home, but America offered no waiting list to education and a dollar whose value would provide. So with a dollar and a prayer my parents left their parents and siblings to board a plane headed towards a future for their children. My father arrived first. He shared floor space with other dreamers; their heads also filled with images of grandeur from magazines and movies. He worked jobs that traditional Americans believed beneath their threshold. The jobs they did not want. That a government told them "they" took. With these same jobs he cobbled together the money for a plane ticket and he sent for my mother. A woman with an eighth grade traditional education that pales in comparison to the life lessons she learned navigating the waters of a foreign sea. They arrived on a stranger's land. Their accents and dress were greeted with a mocking tongue and looks of contempt. They had resolve though. Hella. I watched my parents work jobs beneath their dreams and capacity. All in sacrifice for my sister and for myself. We were not rich by any stretch. We braved cold Chicago nights in the winter with hot food in our bellies. We made do, mom could find stamps for sale in a snow storm. She'd buy your stamps but she would never accept your handout. One of the earliest memories from my childhood is of my parents working. Incessantly. My mother a cashier/beauty consultant at Walgreens. My father a shoes salesman at Florsheim by day, and an overnight cashier at 7-11 by night, did so without complaint. I remember my father getting laid off and going back to school to be a Renal

Dialysis Technician. He ran on four hours sleep. On weekends he cut the grass, cleaned the gutters, and washed the cars. He took care of the outside and my mother took care of the inside. Mom was no slouch. She worked that job for 33 years and retired without fanfare. The company like most companies barely showed appreciation, for time served. She ran the household expertly. She made sure we were clothed, fed, and that we knew we were loved. She would go without the pleasantries and the fancy things. More sacrifice. All for our collective. I remember my father going to work after foot surgery. We woke to a trail of bloody footprints leading to the door. He did not have the sick days left to take off, but rent was due. He worked two jobs while the sutures bled. Modeling the importance of hard work. Men from his generation spent off days painting houses and landscaping lawns. Proud of the homes and families they built. I watched how they lived and modeled character with zero reward, just the satisfaction of family. The success of their children was evidence enough of their planning and labor. I watched people make fun of my mother's accent and confuse her basic understanding of the English language as her level of intellect. She would talk to me in (French) and three other dialects (Twi, Ga & Fanti) the importance of integrity. My sister, six years older than I, was at U of I in Champaign. She moved out when I was 12. We do not talk much, only when necessary, but ours was a relationship of needs, not wants. Ninety percent of my family was overseas and I had never had a soul food Sunday dinner. My grandparents died before I could meet them. I had never had a Big Mama or "Madea". I had no recipes to look forward to on holidays. I lost most of my uncles and aunts. I had the Big Three though. Mom, dad, and my sister. That was it. Like most, I did not appreciate them like I should have growing up. Flowers while they are alive and what not. That is your first network you know? The ones who are there despite circumstances. Not until I got older did I realize that they were the only unconditional stakeholders in my life. They were committed to my ascension even before I was. Even if they did not show it in the way I wanted them. Though we wanted the Huxtables, the Evans lessons were blessings. We grew up poor and without much, but we certainly always had enough. We had lights. We had water and we had love. We were on our own for Jordan brand gym shoes, but we never went without what was necessary to be successful. We were given the tools to prosper and the freedom to apply them in a city with a history of iron will and blue collars.

"Memories on corners with the fo's and the mo's
Walk to the store for the rose, talking straightforward to hoes
Got uncles that smoke, and some put blow up they nose
To cope with the lows, the wind is cold and it blows…"
Common - The Corner

Chicago is the city that chiseled me and molded my resolve. Chicago, with its civil rights history, music just as blue and as soulful as a Langston Hughes poem, and foods as flavorful as the people digesting it, bred my demeanor. The black slaves who migrated from the south and made their way here gave me my center. Bus rides through Auburn Gresham, Englewood, and Roseland communities on the way to the lake after soaking in the black excellence of Hyde Park was a tapestry of pure emotions driven by bucket boys. Joining in the debates of Uncle Remus vs. Harold's, but the whole time championing Reese's on 87th. Getting a walking taco from any corner store in the hood when the "elotes man" was out of corn. The grilled onions from Maxwell's bridging the North and South sides. I grew up down the street from Jeremiah Wright's Trinity United Church of Christ. I graduated valedictorian from St. Thaddeus Elementary school down the way from Harlan and 95 MOB. I wore Pro-Wings and XJ900s. I hustled to buy my first pair of name brand gym shoes. Adidas Street Wise. I grew up dark skinned in the late 80's/early 90's when they only made space for Big Daddy Kane and Wesley Snipes, and my mother cut my hair with scissors. I could read though. I would read. Everything. I was valedictorian in 8th grade and I thought my smart ass could outsmart the world. I was on my way to one of the best high schools in the country and I was already over it. I was 13 and I hung with 18 and 19 year olds with cars and studio apartments. Real baller shit I thought. I could not wait to grow up and get a job and have my own money and do what I wanted with it. I mean, that is what being grown up was, right? I remember growing sideburns that in the right light looked like I had a beard. I, like most teenagers, wanted to look like my idols on TV. I wanted to be Aaron Hall with the New Jack Swing face. My father told me to cut it, and me being me, I was defiant. I would sneak in my father's closet, borrowing clothes, trying to fast forward past the years I now wish I fully embraced.

One day, I was coming home from St. Thaddeus Elementary and I had to cross tracks between neighborhoods. Correction. I had to cross tracks between two rival gang territories. I remember getting chased home all the while screaming that I was only 13 years old. In high school, I had not learned my lesson and was still anxious. I could not wait for the day that I would be grown. Whatever the hell that meant. I was tired of being dictated to, following orders, and everyone telling me they knew what was best for me. I was sick of being on an adult calendar and schedule, doing chores and homework that I found stupid. I knew I was going to be rich and in charge. Whatever the hell that meant. I was not a kid anymore. I did not need to be reminded of hygiene or have my lunch made. I had no idea that I was at the most important stage of my life. I call it the transitional years. This was the time to make constructive, not destructive mistakes, and embrace constructive criticisms. This is the time to seek mentorship and opportunities to learn.

I was old enough to be trusted with responsibilities. I was mature enough to have my integrity tested. I did not recognize this at this age. I just wanted to have fun. I was ready to get high school over with and do what? I had no idea what it took to be a grown up and really had no plan for life after high school except go to college. I knew school. It was comfortable and I was complacent. I mismanaged this time of my life. Like most teenagers, I thought I knew more than I did. I thought a surface understanding of something was knowledge about it. I, like most of you, had been programmed to think life came into you in yearly increments. It is soooooo not. You get accustomed to graduations and birthdays. You have 8th grade & high school graduation and your sweet sixteen's. Life gives you finish lines at first. Then, it does not. I got the gist of things in my haste to be grown. There was no depth to my mastery. I had not truly understood the value of time and how to use it wisely. I was in rush. Do not do this.

"I'm from where the beef is inevitable, Summertime's unforgettable
Boosters in abundance, buy a half-price sweater new
Your word was everything, so everything you said you'd do.
You did it, couldn't talk about it if you ain't lived it..."
S. Carter - Where I'm from

I arrived at Whitney Young by train unpolished and unrefined. My first revelation of my limited experience, no my limited exposure, were the conversations I had with the other teenagers I met when I got there. They were not like my local crew. They had means. Their parents had contacts. They had been places and wore clothes and shoes that cost a light bill. Meanwhile, I had a job at Walgreens (thanks to mom) and gave my check to my parents for our light bill. I saw my classmates getting dropped off in luxury cars while I rode the bus and trains. I heard the music of my city before it became the soundtrack of popular culture. Lonnie before Common. Kanye before the Kardashians. I had not figured out who I was or what I was to become. Like most people, I feigned certainty as I searched for footing. I tried on different costumes. They never fit. I spent the majority of my time being cool and accessible as opposed to being my natural self. I was consumed with the gossip of the day, the new shoe, song, or who was fighting at lunch. None of this mattered. I should have been more self-serving and used school for what it was for; practice for the real world.

I did not recognize the opportunity to make constructive mistakes. Instead, I perpetuated the teacher versus student narrative. I just wanted to be grown. I was smart, but I was not studious. I graduated with a 2.89 and a 26 on the ACT just missing out on scholarships. I wanted out of the house so I could be grown. This was the only reason I committed to college. Freedom. Nobody told me you only go if it is part of the plan and not because it was the bigger school after high school. I honestly went away to school to get away from home, not family necessarily. My environment did not offer much. I had not seen much. I figured college would be my ticket out of the crib. My dorm would be my first apartment. My meal plan offered three meals. So I had three hot's and a cot. The institutionalization of it all. The irony. High school was vital to my development. It was my exploratory phase like it was for most youth. When I should have been planning and making those constructive mistakes, I skipped or skated in class. I took a B when an A was right there. I cut classes to hang with friends I had not known for two months, but they had a car, and I had five on whatever. My drive was seeing the city. I graduated .11 points away from a scholarship that would have paid for my future had I not wanted to see the views. Had I not chosen to take myself for granted, the time spent holding on to childish ways, I could have invested in a head start for my grown self. I would have been more prepared for that bigger school after high school.

College was the escape remember? I finessed my way to Tennessee State University. Big Band. Big Concerts. Big Fun. Bigger responsibilities. I signed up for contractual indentured servitude in the form of student loans; because of those .11 GPA points, I sat in classes where I was clearly smarter but also not prepared. I learned my lesson the hard way. That lesson was this: This is the time. You do not get any more of it. All that time plodding and "could not wait—ing" to be an adult. I could have got ready. Do not rush the responsibility before the preparation. Even in my rush to look older, I was not ready for the responsibility that comes with being older. All the time lost appealing for a different look, I could have spent that time learning to love me instead. Why be in a rush to look older and be older? You are older way longer than you are young. Embrace it. I needed time. I needed to prepare. I needed to look at time as a commodity, not something for reserve. Invest time in yourself. Time is more valuable than anything you could imagine. Value it. The clock never stops running. And it is always running out.

Careful what you wish for you might receive it, " he
said... Then B.I. said, "Hov' remind yourself
Nobody built like you, you designed yourself"
I agree I said, my one of a kind self
Get stoned every day like Jesus did
What he said, I said, has been said before
"Just keep doing your thing, " he said, say no more..."
S. Carter — A Dream

I orchestrated my escape. Pretty soon I was off to Nashville. It was 1998 and I was at Tennessee State University one of the most renowned HBCUs. I was finally away from home. It was a haberdashery of blackness from all corners of the globe. It was my first venture outside of Chicago. I had $1000 saved in an account, my school supplies and toiletries, boxes of ramen and cereal, a microwave, TV, and a suitcase. I said I would never look back. I was so anxious to get out on my own, that I got to the dormitory days early and slept on the hard cold floor. I was anxious and ill prepared. I barely went to classes. I partied. I drank. I danked. I definitely gained weight. I remember we had a dorm versus dorm water fight with water guns, water balloons, wet towels, and socks. You name it, we wet it, and threw it at each other. There were concerts with major artists like Beyonce´ and 'nem (I kid, I kid). I snuck in to see the Hard Life Tour with Jay-Z when it came to our campus. I was at every ice cream social, barbeque, house party, and kickback. I saw all of the fraternities and sororities and waited my turn.

All of this had me too tired for class and my performance started to show. I was having a tough time being disciplined. I had never needed to be. I would always get by or get the B in the clutch. I had never had to apply myself. Now the adulthood I swore I could not wait for was here and I was getting exposed. I was having way too much fun with the freedom I had instead of recognizing the advantage I was afforded. I had zero major responsibilities and a ton of time. I had time to plan, network, and organize for success, but I was too busy picking fits for the parties. I had to be at all the events, feeling left out if I missed. Popularity mattered, my coolness had to be the coolest. I had 100% attendance at all things fun and was shooting for 50% at all things that mattered. I had not yet learned how to determine what had value in the long run. Fun was immediate and satisfying. Work was well, work. I did not want any of that.

The thing is you cannot avoid it, you simply delay it. Whether I was ready or not, life was knocking at the door. Opportunities abound. My lack of planning and haste had me run out of money in a month, face the threat of academic probation, get held up by gunpoint for a few hours (long em effing story), lose grants, and waste time at a very fun school. A school that was also losing accreditation at the time (meaning my degree would be worth about a dollar). I was almost 20 years old and not a kid anymore. I had not accomplished anything since graduation. I was still working part time jobs, hustling to get by, or figuring out how to get over. I was going from the dorm during the school year, to the bedroom I lost my virginity in during the summers. This did nothing for my self-esteem. Not to mention, I could no longer afford to be out of state. I had no idea what to do about any of it. Life told me to grow up. Ready or not, I had to figure out how to grow up and I already felt behind. I had made some wonderful memories. Had a lot of fun. I had not used my time wisely at all. I still had no plan for success. At twenty years old, I was headed to Bloomington. I transferred to Illinois State University to be closer to home. I needed my foundation.

"The new moon rode high in the crown of the metropolis
Shining, like, "Who on top of this?"
People was tusslin', arguing and bustlin'
Gangstas of Gotham hardcore hustlin'
I'm wrestling with words and ideas
My ears is pricked, seeking what will transmit
The scribes can apply to transcript…"
Mos Def - Respiration

Remember I mentioned how you were programmed to deal with life in birthdays and graduations? Well I was at another of my graduations. I finished the bigger school and I had a degree that I did not want. I was heading home to Chicago. After college, I was back at Walgreens. I was a manager and I hated it. I was still unpolished and unrefined. I still had the workings of a plan but no actual plan to work. The money was good but without a plan, the money came and went. Stuff kept me busy. Nothing of value. Just stuff. Games, electronics all of it. Chasing after it too. We grew up poor so like most poor people, I hid my economic status with stuff. Now that I was making my own money, Jordans, PlayStations, clothes, phones, and restaurants all got a piece of my check. I had not yet learned the value of money. I knew cash. I knew how to count. I got the "save money", two word financial plan from my parents so I thought a savings account and a shoebox was the move. I knew I wanted things and the temporary pleasure it gave me when purchased.

The acquisition of things is a fleeting feeling though. It is also a very isolated experience. It was my money. It was my car. It was my place. It was my toys. I could not tell you where one of those cars is, who lives in that apartment, or where those toys are today. I had either outgrown the clothes or they became outdated before I had time to wear them. Hell some clothes came back in style before I remembered ever purchasing them. I had all this stuff, but nothing of value. I was no closer to that dream car or dream house. I did not have a mortgage, but I still had bills. I still had a car to gas up, insurance to pay, and a cell phone bill. I took all of this for granted and then I was fired (another long em effing story). I remember the only job I could get was selling office supplies store to store. The meetings would go like this. Me: "blah blah blah so you want to purchase office supplies?" Them: "Nah, Office Depot or Staples has a sale." It was humiliating. It was humbling.

I knew then more than ever I needed to start my plan. I was back living at home, with all this stuff, and back in the bedroom where I lost my virginity. Tragic. I was still buying stuff. I still was insecure about every decision I made. I still relied on external validation and had no instincts. I could see the confidence in my peers and was covetous. I was on a journey that I thought I was on alone. I had no idea that everyone I knew was searching for their reason to exist. It is a wonderful thing to be certain of your purpose. Meeting the milestones of validation that says you are intentional. That your work is worthy and that every culminating effort that drives your feet has value. I had not experienced that lesson yet. I was aimless. I thought: this is life. That greatness is for the anointed. Like most people I accepted my present station in life as everlasting.

I had to learn that people change and then change their circumstances. It is allowed. In order to tailor my plan for success, I became a student of myself. It was important to approach this academically. It was important to have that youthful exuberance like the first day of school and your new clothes. I readied myself. I dressed for it. I realized that there exists people who are using their time to advance themselves. People who place themselves in situations and environments that lead to a greatness simply by using what they had and who they knew to get ahead. I began to learn my strengths, weaknesses, and how to improve them. I took account of what I had and what I needed. These were the most important steps I could take, and like a baby's first steps, they would highlight the beginning of the journey of my lifetime. I would identify where I could go for free information, the awesomeness of technology, and any tool I could imagine to sharpen my acumen. That simply meant trying to improve my skill set and utility.

I had to become brave in the face of failure and avoid the comfort of the easy win. Trying to become self-aware by maximizing what I knew and learning what I did not was not easy. This had to happen though.1) I could be less reliant and be independent and 2) I would have more control over my time with this independence. As I refined myself, I strove to maximize me. I searched for footing and I strategized. I developed and along the way I took notes. This is what I found. People are miserable without purpose. Empty and unsure of their place. It is like trying on different suits and understandably being displeased with the fit. When you find the right suit though? You are dressed for all occasions and I was finding my suit.

"See, I'm influenced by the ghetto you ruined
The same dude you gave nothin', I made somethin' doin'
What I do, through and through and
I give you the news with a twist, it's just his ghetto point of view..."
S. Carter - Renegade

There was a time when I did not have all that stuff. Everybody had the 8 bit Nintendo with the PowerGlove and Zapper in their rooms. They all had Starter jackets, Jordans, and Girbaud jeans. I remember having the chicken pox and my family having me damn near quarantined in my room. My father would open the door, slide a tray of food in, throw a comic on the bed, and close the door before I could blink. Comics became my only refuge during that time. Marvel over DC of course. It is a no brainer. I would read them over and over infatuated with the artwork and stories. When I was not reading them, I had pen and paper. I taught myself how to draw comic book quality characters through trial and error. Learning how to shape bodies and define muscles, I could would draw characters, fabricating my own black superheroes. I would pen their stories and shape their lives. I would practice at this craft daily. I simply loved to draw.

I remember my father taking me to my first auto show in Chicago. The place was huge. I saw every luxury car I could. Like everybody growing up, I dreamed of owning a car at 16. I liked cars. Scratch that, I loved them. I got in the driver seat and played with all the knobs, bells and whistles. I grabbed brochures by the volume. I would read everything I could. I would talk for hours about it to anybody who would listen. All the car guys my father knew, mechanics, truck drivers, anybody who did anything automobile related, I annoyed them with questions to pick their brains. What connects both of these stories is that my interests were peaked like never before. What affects my effort was attributed to interest. Simply put, effort is correlated by interest. I tried only if I cared. I needed to find something to connect, to some reason to engage. If it fed me somehow or stoked my passions, I would work incessantly. The effort required however, is correlated to interest and passion. It is easier to work towards an interest and a passion.

It is difficult following the popular opinion of what the audience thinks works for you, when you do not care anything about the thing they claim works. Your effort will start to feel grueling and weighted because you simply are not vested in what you are doing. You are toiling. If the work that you are doing is not part of the plan, your end game, or even a means to an end you had ever even envisioned for yourself, it is almost insanity. Exhaust yourself for an end that justifies your usage. Identifying your passions will help you determine where best to invest time and energy. This effectively and efficiently uses your efforts towards mastery. Those who identify where their passions lie, use their energies towards mastery of concepts about their interests that increases the confidence to walk within their purpose. The sooner I realized this, the sooner I was able to reap the benefit.

Passions are personal. This allows for tailoring and mapping your plan to your size as opposed to a plan from the audience that is one size fits all. This is the thought process necessary to manage expectations when comparing your progression to others as your knowledge base and interpretations develop. I get it. We all peek over the fence. We check the room for competition, but we also use our peers and foes as a barometer. I would ask myself "what does this person and myself have in common"? What am I comparing? Experience? Skills? What exactly? Ask yourself, are your passions and interests similar to the person you deem the litmus test for your life? Who and what are you comparing yourself to, before you jump from the ledge or abandon your plan.

Once I was able to pull myself from the ledge, I gathered by dissecting these comparisons. I would see that I was doing myself a huge disservice. I was comparing my chapter 1, (Hell my Introduction) to someone else's chapter 12. People are on different stretches of their journey and with that, skill sets will differ, acquisition of knowledge will occur at different times, and the truth reached will be personal. These comparisons are dangerous because you see the output, not the input, nor the sacrifice. You fall in love with the splendor not the rigor. People love watching the highlights, but you should watch the workouts too. The revelation of success often makes success appear instantaneous. The accomplishment is celebrated in its present form. The milestones along the way are not. We celebrate at the finish line instead of after each training session we crush. They are often ignored. There are no overnight successes. You cannot avoid the work. Even the effort to expedite steps in the process of success requires effort. It takes work to skip steps. You know how much energy and time is wasted in avoiding work that is inevitable? People seek work they are comfortable doing. Chores that fit comfortably within their skill set. They want to gain muscles but seek a comfortable weight to lift. A distance they can walk that is not too far. A career that does not require much of them. It is in the application where your truth is discovered. As you prepare and acquire skills it is in the application of what is practiced where the truth is found. That is, as you develop, you theorize your culmination, you dream of the end. Until what you have learned after application and practice is validated or invalidated the lens of your belief or valuation will be cloudy. You will learn something, try it, it will work, or it will not. You will now know. This is increase. This truth or falsehood is personal. You have a belief of who you are and what you believe of yourself is validated by actions. If you believe you are noble, but your actions are without integrity, your truth is invalid. The valuation of the plan for success is determined through application, trial and error, passing or failing. Either you is or you ain't and there is only one way to prove it.

The ability to articulate why, suggests depth of understanding of what your purpose is. You will refine your idea through articulation. Speaking with purpose, being intentional in stating what your goals are will serve you well. This practice, over time becomes your mantra. You can clearly state your personal mission statement. This becomes habitual and with that the confidence of certainty. So while you are saying your mantra and other ideologies are introduced, if you cannot fit these new sentences into the paragraph of your mantra, then it does not fit. You will become rest assured that your steps are becoming ordered. This is the calming of preparedness. It is that confidence that makes governing your life with certainty real. You will begin to say your plan as a manifesto to those who you entrust that will listen. You will become what you preach. This is what being real is. This is where confidence lies. This confidence is often exhibited by the educated. There exists the misnomer that education only implies college educated or solely book smart. It does not. Your intellectual capacity is not solely defined by a GPA.

Your genius does not come from a book. It comes from your experiences. The experiences that form a frame of reference are absolutely valuable for your understanding and increased knowledge. I continuously take account of what I know, what I learned, and most definitely where I am, in my process of progression. It is imperative. I have to accommodate new knowledge and new experiences. The use of prior knowledge allows for advantages in attempts at mastery. Mastery is effected as it depends on when you are introduced to the topic, your expressed interest, your passion and time invested. Logically, if you are strategically exposed to the subject at hand before your competition and peers, you have a distinct advantage. If that expressed interest is fostered, it thrives. If time is spent in practice and application, it soars. In academia, even at work, people with low grades, poor acclimation to institutional and or societal constructs, assume their peers with the converse skills love waking up early, writing papers and studying for tests as a past time. Let us be clear. They do not. Not at all. In many instances, control over the variables of mastery is a rarity to have. This causes many to unfairly interpret their shortcomings as innate. They are not. Many people blame all of their shortcomings on some made up defect. "I'm not smart, that is why I'm not good at math." If you have not been introduced to a concept and have had no time to practice toward mastery how can you possibly be expected to produce? Because this concept is missed, the difficulties many people face allow for what they feel are justifiable reasons to disengage and thusly, not practice. They then reconcile by diminishing the value of the challenge. Statements such as, "the class is stupid, the company is stupid, the work is stupid," attribute weight. This suggests that it is all in the valuation. Valuation determines your contributive efforts towards mastery. What are you willing to do for you? How much do you value you? It is in the variables that affect mastery where the disparities in success lie for an individual. Your understanding of to what degree they can be influenced and how, is how you resolve to continue their pursuit of success. Why do some people seem to get it? How do they recognize what they need to work on, while others do not. Why the work seems easier for others and for some difficult. They understand to what degree they can influence the variables and those they cannot. They realize that the one constant they can control is themselves and their knowledge. I am a work in progress until the day that I die. So are you. I had to learn that. Learning is continuous. It does not plateau. You do not ever get full from the feast that is education. You never get dulled on the flavor of information. Know where you are, where you want to go, and plot out how to get there. Every single day.

"Struggle another sign that God love you
'Cause on the low
Being poor make you humble
Keep they names in my rhymes
To try and keep 'em out of trouble
'Cause being poor also teach you how to hustle"
Lupe Fiasco — Real

My first step was observing the greats and what screamed at me was that I had to increase my knowledge base. I saw other people doing the same. When I quieted the noise and put the stuff down, I was able to see who was really doing and who was only talking. I saw some of the talkers were just that, talkers. Some were practicing their sales pitch and others, they were excited to tell what they knew about what someone else was doing to anyone who would listen. I saw those who do, do it well, and a quite few fail. Both looked like forward progress while the rest stood still. I got some of the best lessons from just observing. I still do. I understand that in our quest for our supreme self we are all at different stages of the journey. Those doing it well at some point were just talkers who had a sales pitch and initially their efforts at success failed. They became successful because they would not accept any other possibility. They respected the necessity of failure and what you learn from it. Something motivated them. Intrinsically or externally. I had to look inward. For me to truly grow, I had to be honest with myself. I had to really understand my motives, my interests, my tolerances, my biases, my passions, my fears and my weaknesses. I had to determine what I knew, what I did not know, and why I did not know it. I had to confront my bullshit. My role in my present state. Not taking school seriously, ditching classes, picking parties over class participation. I had to sit down and proclaim what was my fault and what was I going to do about it. I had to accept my truths. The advantage is this is a personal and private experience. I could have these conversations with myself and hold a mirror up. Privately. In my own big ass head. No worry about the audience, lights, and cameras. No bother by the opinion of friends and family. Silent conversations with self. Reflection. In these moments, running from my truths is not possible. Only then I could begin to arm myself with the knowledge I needed to affect my greatness. Only then I could develop my plan for success. I was ready for it. I was ready to go after what I claimed I deserved. In my search for sure footing, I would be frustrated at the amount of information to which I was ignorant. No. The more I researched and saw not only what

I did not know but some of the circumstantial advantages I was not afforded because of whatever economic, social-emotional, societal construct in front of me, I would be alt-right pissed off. I mean out right. After all of the emotion of how much I was ignorant to, I would want to blame someone, anyone for my shortcomings. I was also honestly scared. I was too afraid to admit my responsibility. My part in this. How I did not try. How I waited to feel like doing it. How I waited for a savior. It would be overwhelming sometimes and made the idea of becoming anything besides what I already was feel like an impossibility. It made the weight of being more than my family or what my environment suggested of me seem too much to carry. It was easier to accept the present me I knew over a future that I could picture but not touch. I had no paint brushes or canvas to paint what I saw for myself. The confidence to believe that I could was not always there. It was crazy. I would watch the success stories of some of my favorite artists, musicians, designers and the influencers. They all had a dollar and a dream story. I had a dollar. I had a dream. I can bet a buck on me. Here I was filling this void with stuff, not realizing that I had everything I needed to begin pursuing my dreams. Hell, I started to see how much I missed out and how much time I had lost without a plan. I needed to begin planning for success and not just waiting on it. I simply reminded myself that other artists had to develop their craft. Other people had to become great as well. I began to pay attention to what made people successful. I needed to know why people understood concepts or had a familiarity with notions that I struggled to grasp. I needed to understand why people were further along in their plan than I was. I became a student of human behavior. In all of this I learned that it is in everyone to be considered great, to scale. Environment and nurturement influence the manifestation of this greatness in dramatic ways. Almost incalculable detriment or advantage can be affected by a quality environment and the right people in your network. You may not have the greatest home, be from the greatest neighborhood, and this most definitely sucks. You may not have the best familial structure, the most favorable financial situation or even the know-how, yet and this also sucks. What you do have is your honest self. This is your advantage. I grew up poor on the South side of post-industrial Chicago. That is important to denote because this gave rise to the high rises and gang violence. You had to watch hands and listen to how quick the volume changed in conversation. You had to know a little bit of every gang lit and hand shake to navigate gang turfs. It was important to know who called it over where and what bus to get off on at what time. I was left to my own devices. Recap. My parents were immigrants figuring the nuances of a new country. My older sister was busy during her own formative years. My father worked two jobs and my mother with functional English ran the household. With that duality of being a first generation Ghanaian-American and a black boy in Chicago, I had to figure most things out on my own, as my network had no prior experience to draw from. I could not let my circumstances, limited advocates, language barriers prevent me from surviving. And that was instinctive. You instinctively preserve yourself. You instinctively survive. You instinctively search for the ideal conservation, how to best retain resources. That is how I know greatness is within. I began to pay attention to the people I admired. I appreciated that everything they did gave me insight to who they were. I soon understood that everything that a person does is feedback for me to process and make determinations about who I was dealing with. People reveal themselves through action and thusly are defined in action, not in theory. The assumption of who any one is has not yet been validated until we witness them apply the characteristics of who we think they are. Do their actions match their speech? Do they live by the words they stress? Does the owner of Ford drive one as he pushes Fords on the populous? Would he let his kids drive it? What you do defines you, not what you say. I began to watch for those who relied on the backs of others for labor while not being committed to working for themselves. They had an excuse readily available, scapegoats at their behest. How could they advise me or give directives to others? They have not done a thing to attribute weight to their words. Why when they do not even want it enough for themselves to try to be great should I listen to their belief about my ascension? After all, that is really all it takes to be great, consistent effort at each opportunity to apply the knowledge you acquire. You learn from each application and each time you are moving toward your greatness. Love your struggle, it is building you.

"Beware the false motives of others
Be careful of those who pretend to be brothers
And you never suppose it's those who are closest to you
To you They say all the right things, to gain their position
Then use your kindness as their ammunition
To shoot you down in the name of ambition, they do…"
Lauryn Hill — Forgive Them Father

I never joined a gang though I knew who I knew and who I was supposed to know. I was 14 hanging with crews filled with 19 and 21 year olds trying to emulate who they were, not knowing who I was yet. They all had the stuff that I wanted though. It was appealing and enough to attract me. I flirted with Chicago's underbelly but I did not get eaten. I was able to see how all the folks I looked up to had a role to fill for the good of the gang. They all had "OG's" and "Big Bro's". They were shown that if they played their positions and when the timing was right they too could become the man themselves. Even on this path they had resources to turn to and people to lean on. They had a steward to guide them to their peril. I had not learned how to use discernment. I was lucky though. I was able to see many of these "friends" make mistakes and some of them make it. I had that frame of reference at least. I saw how they worked the gang dynamic. I was at Whitney Young and got the opportunity to see that same gang dynamic applied in groups for positive ends. I began to see how important discernment was to the development of your network and acceptance of leadership even at work. There are bosses and there are leaders. I have worked for many of the former because the latter is rare. The former sucks. I had all the ambition and pluck but no real direction yet. I had an idea of where I wanted to go and not necessarily how to get there. I was still watching those who were doing what I wanted or on their way. I had a boss who I thought because of his position could lead me or at the very least guide me to the promised land. He did not. Instead he stole my ideas and trumpeted them as his own. He stifled my development and used my youthful exuberance and lack of direction against me to his gain. Now, here I was headed to college on my Dollar and a Dream, J. Cole vibe and I realized this, college without a mentor and your team is trash. I had the realization that I could not get to my destination in a vacuum. I did not come from a big ass family, at least stateside. I knew Jordan had Scottie. Hall had Oates. Wu had Tang. Your favorite rappers, favorite rapper has a team behind the curtains. Your favorite beauty has a stylist. I needed that same support. It was so clear. You can only improve the efficiency of your learning curve through networking. Common ground is the security of the Human experience. It connects us. Our interests categorize us. We are separated and unified by our camaraderie, discord, and interests. As we differ across a spectrum of interests, our quest for originality is almost incessant. This ironically makes us fundamentally the same.

We all seek fulfillment. What that is and how it may manifest differs for every individual. That thirst for purpose, that thirst to be used for something more is not unique. We all want to be valuable. In that we serve. It is in this longing for belonging we associate ourselves with people who we deem as extensions of us. We connect and formulate organizations and societal structures to further connect to something larger than we could be alone. All of this to increase our odds of success. These relationships are necessary to your development. Creating quality relationships is key to your growth. A network of qualified individuals who can expose you to those lessons you need to equip yourself with for ascension is how you will maximize your potential. The quality of your network can be correlated to the humility you are willing to express. You simply cannot be the smartest person in the room. Improvement over ego. You must acquire knowledge from people who have traversed waters you plan to navigate. This is the importance of humility. The importance of listening to wisdom. Wisdom is specific to experience. It is not chronologically activated. I mean just because you get older, you do not necessarily get smarter. Though networking is vital, you cannot leave your success in the hands of anyone. Your vision. Your baby. Accountability is personal. You design yourself. It is quintessential to maximizing your realization. Of the steps that make success that much more attainable, being able to hold yourself accountable is singularly the most difficult and important task. Your efforts cannot be excused by the lack of contributory measures of others toward your triumph. Your success. Your responsibility. Deal with it. Learning how to trust others and lean on them was foreign to me. This was hard. Managing personalities is demanding. Especially because people can be jerks. So many situations call for you to process and react to people and their mentality. Their frame of reference. Instantly. Doing your best to understand people in a specific context allows you to engage with them is the best way to manage your expectations. This taught me that you must use discernment to determine who is a protagonist in the story of your life.

The intention of an individual will dictate their agenda. One's motive gives to reason. Simply put, why are people around you? Why do you keep people around? What do they want? What do you want? What you want or what you value determines how you should act and with whom you should associate. Your actions should be purposeful. Your efforts measured. Be careful of your influences. The only influence of value is what motivates your ascension. These influences do not breed apprehension. They do not foster doubt. Fear is infectious. It can even be disguised as concern but if the concern births fear, this can impede your efforts. This does little to serve your plan. Influence should be inspirational. Be leery of who you allow access to you. Your ideas, your beliefs, your goals, your purpose. They are to be guarded. Stop sharing your vision with people who cannot see what you see. They will convince you that what you are seeing is merely an illusion, when it simply is the foresight of a plan you have yet to enact. That dream is real. You are dreaming for a reason. You are longing for a reason. You are searching for a reason. That reason is your purpose. As you approach your greatness you will be exposed to various lines of thought. You now must become your own steward. Navigating the discourse of dissenting thought. As your plan matures and as ideas come to fruition, you will have had ample time to apply what you have learned and reflect. You will become more confident in your steps. This is the power of discernment. You are NEO in the Matrix now. Your movements deliberate. You are your plan. As I said our commonalities suggest we are closer and far more similar than our differences convey. We all fundamentally want the same; success, but our individuality makes the success personal. Take for example personal finances. If I were to use a measurable, analogous comparison, every person has different definitions of what rich and or wealthy means which indicates that success is subjective. Which is why comparing your gains and losses to others can be detrimental if not metered accordingly. The comparison as part of the reflective process (in this case finances) is personal. Comparing yourself to others using their achievements as the standard for your life goals is just not logical. It is detrimental to the psyche to live in the shadow of envy. You should be inspired by the ascension of others and this should foster your intrinsic motivation to be great. It should make you want to go get yours for you. Worry about yourself.

"Nobody's workin' as hard as you."
And even though I laugh it off, man, it's probly true
'Cause while all of my closest friends out partyin'
I'm just here makin' all the music that they party to..."
Drake-Light it Up

Learning can be inactive. Mastery is not. Learning is the work. Now this is the caveat missed by most. This is unavoidable. The vast majority of people get the gist of something, the overarching objective, or the surface point. They believe this is the same as understanding. It is not. My reading your bio gives me the gist of who you are, but how deep does it go for understanding what made, the truth of you who you are. Be thorough in thought, in process and in application. Anything else is not mastery. We often get caught in the rush of life. This false sense of urgency to do things fast as opposed to doing them thoughtfully. This is why most people have a surface level understanding because they valued the answer more than the logic. True knowledge happens in the nuances necessary to arrive at that the truth. Planning for success is by no means a small task but the reward is valuable beyond measure. This preparedness allows for better mastery of expectations. This education of self is what leads to confidence in self. By always committing to the process, starting with needs assessment, the better equipped you will be at managing your expectations. This needs-based assessment is a logical, reflective approach that allows for proactive measures towards milestones of accomplishment. Figure out what you do not know. Determine your need. With this, you have initialized a plan to learn and address your short comings by simply being honest with yourself. The powerful thing is it is personal. It is private. Be selfish. Tell yourself all the secrets of success you find for refinement. Life does not guarantee your success, however as you navigate your path you realize life is certainly about increasing the odds of success. Absolutely. There is absolutely no room for complacency when becoming great. You must develop your methodology. Methodology is the science of identifying the best practices for the best results. The how to, if you will, for achieving any goal. This is reflective and in this you are to make productive mistakes and accept constructive criticisms. Maturation is in the details. The fine tooth combing of your plan is important. It is also continuous. It aids in mastery. This mastery is correlated to the confidence of the successful. There is no luck. There is only planning for success.

Through orchestration and planning you increase their odds of success. This is advantageous. This fortuitous situation affords you the opportunity to position yourself for success. The better equipped to manage disappointments; to manage failures. This allows for regrouping and adjusting for success. Accommodating success is vital. It is necessary to prepare for the abundance you have earned. Trial and error affords the individual the opportunity to assess their progress. Like, where did I go wrong? How can I fix it so THAT does not happen again? It's learning from your mistakes. This is what is meant by reflective. When recognizing an opportunity to apply knowledge for practice and deeper absorption you will face failures. It is an inevitability. It will be in these moments you are sharpened. You must be willing to make mistakes. Perfection is an aspiration never achieved, but in its pursuit a wealth of knowledge is gathered. There is no loss in learning regardless whether the efforts were successful or the goal achieved. These productive mistakes lead to constructive thought. Solution oriented thinking. Here is where you take notes, adjust, and tailor your plan to your success. Creating personal organizational structures to help you navigate situations is necessary. Discipline means you care. There is no luck. There is only preparation for opportunities. Recognizing opportunities to increase your pallet, diversifying your portfolio so to speak, ensures you have as many tools as possible for your utility belt. People often run from difficulty not realizing the flip side is opportunity. Think about how many businesses were started because groups of people had problems and one guy came up with a solution? He recognized the opportunity others did not. Keep your head on a swivel. Leaders are not common. Leadership takes work and a continuum of increased effort towards your objective. The culmination of these efforts results in goals achieved. That is success. The reward for effort is often immeasurable, but it is the acquisition of the small rewards as well as the large ones that amounts to success. True leaders research, apply thought, develop methodology, create policy, and face the repercussions whether it be to their liking or not. They recognize that this is all part of the process and simplicity of success. They embrace accountability. Followers are lazy and have difficulty recognizing that the process of progress can be disjointed. They do not trust their capabilities. They have not developed their utility belt. They are discouraged by the work required and readily look for reasons to accept their fears. They avoid accountability and come readied with excuses to avoid applying themselves. Followers wait for popular opinion though it may defy all that they see as logical. They appreciate the ease and comfort of not being accountable for the outcome. They are at the mercy of people not vested in their outcome. That is why there are way more followers than leaders. It is safer to hide behind the shield of leadership than to be the tip of the spear as the leader. The varying degrees of success people experience can be attributed to their valuation systems. The ability to connect their efforts to their gains is directly correlated to them continuously giving effort. This is where a steward is necessary, a mentor if you will, until you develop the resolve necessary to thrive between gains. This is the importance of recognizing roles of the influential people in your life as you develop. A person who is influential to your life creates value where there is none, rather where none is seen. They are to influence how you think about thinking. This is metacognition. The significance of this relationship is only valuable if it positively influences and manipulates your metacognitive capacities. This means your circle is only as good as what they inspire out of you. The need is to create critical thinkers, not reproductions of their thought. This is how you build leaders. Valuing how you think of content and context as opposed to the production and manifestation of an outcome. Process over product. No robots. It is in this care and attending to the thought process that allows for the connection and buy in with student and master, organization and construct. Gang leader or teacher this consideration conveys a respect for who you are in depth. Receiving this thoughtfulness from your circle is key to ascension. I began to listen with discernment who wanted to give me unbiased opinion and who wanted me to "do it like them." The choice of words people spoken over me began to matter. The people with unlimited yes's and drive as opposed to the bottomless no's and cautious tales discouraging me from even trying. I started to notice the people who hoarded information and the difficulty that came with getting information from them. I contrasted that to the people who would tell me all that they knew and all that had survived. The tones they used. Did they listen or did they dictate? Did they remember things I said or did they simply listen for the gist? When developing my plan for success, recognizing stakeholders, those vested in my outcome, was absolutely important. Nobody wins alone. This is the importance of diplomacy. Diplomacy over politics. It is the ultimate unifier and quintessential to networking. It allows leadership to develop organically. Politics is orchestrated. It is manipulative and requires micromanagement of relationships to insure alliances. Diplomacy is gracious and fosters relationships regardless of agenda because it is pure. It is a movement, not a man.

"Do you believe in me? Are you deceiving me?
Could I let you down easily, is your heart where it need to be?
Is your smile on permanent? Is your vow on lifetime?
Would you know where the sermon is if I died in this next line?
I freed you from being a slave in your mind, you're very welcome
You tell me my song is more than a song, it's surely a blessing
But a prophet ain't a prophet til they ask you this question..."
K. Lamar- Mortal Man

When I was able to align my passions and my personality to a profession, I became an educator. I took all those classes and suffered through all those professional development courses to become a master of my content. Do not get me wrong, I absolutely love technology and computer science and graphic design and blah blah blah. What I loved most of all about teaching was talking to my students about life and their lives beyond the classroom. Beyond being a Lion, a Thunderbird or a Spartan, I loved seeing who they were and who they dreamed of becoming. It was interesting to see how eager students were for the world that awaited them and how ill prepared they were. I recognized the "could not wait" that I had at that age oozing from them. I loved talking to "know- it-all" students basking in their lack of knowledge and understanding, realizing ignorance is truly bliss. They had no idea what was ahead and no idea how little of an idea they had. It was awesome and frightening in the same breath to hear their assumptions about life and their quick fixes and solutions such as "I'm going to get a job and an apartment," and that "100 thousand dollars would be enough for them to retire." Pure comedy. It became part of my duty to impart truth, force maturation, and help students develop a plan for success. One class at a time. I started teaching 13 years ago and my students who were then 16 are now 29 and I often run into them at the gym or out running errands. They stop me and remind me of our conversations and redirection and how my accessibility helped them get through high school. I was simply born to teach. I am the cool teacher. The favorite after the fact. The tough love teacher. You got treated no treats. It is a misconception that the cool teacher lets you get away with murder, on the contrary, I have to be culturally responsive and keep a finger on the pulse of the students I serve. I was new school as the old heads called it. I was simply being myself. I was the same age as most of my students' big bros. I wore the same clothes. I listened to the same music. I lived in the same neighborhoods. I would play that same music during class. Instrumentals of course. Instead of timer for quiz, I'd play producer Zaytoven's instrumentals. I figured they knew how long the song was, so they would know how much time they had left on the quiz. I would stop mid lesson to discuss how I felt Gucci Mane had more impact on the culture than Young Jeezy and listen to their rebuttals. We would have Socratic seminars about how only the "Foamposites" were second to Jordan and that you cannot lose with Air Max 95's. I would have to call out students for false flagging for clout as I knew more lit then they pretended to study. It was important to be cool enough to be relevant, honorable enough to be respected, diplomatic enough to be trusted and competent enough to lead. I would not say much at first, deliberately unnoticed as I observed and assessed the needs of others. Then I would create buy in by "weaponizing" my influence for a positive end. I determine how I am perceived. I use this to positively impact the trajectory of a life in my role. I would often say that I have the same savoir-faire as a gang recruiter, but I love my people more than the profit I would make in their demise. My approach is not practiced. Though I work on my craft for my purpose, my passion is not manufactured. It is not work-shopped. It was not professionally developed. It comes from certainty of who I am and what I stand for. It is innate. It exudes from my walk to my "style and grace..." At the time of this offering I will have been a West African, Ghanaian to be exact, male teacher by profession for 12 years in Chicago and a student forever. In all of education, there is only 2% that represents African American males. 2%. It is true you can misuse your influence. I try hard not to. My music resonates. My clothes resonate. My voice resonates. I do not take this for granted. Being culturally relevant and a tool for progression during the most formative years is a role I embrace. Absolutely. This realization did not come easy. It was not without loss, failure, frustration, embarrassment and the experience I was afforded by it all that revealed my capacities. I had to learn what defined my greatness was my servitude, how I was used, which in essence is how I empowered others. It was simple logic. You have to be powerful to empower. Me helping you achieve greatness, is a manifestation of my own. As an educator this power is knowledge. A resource designed for portability. Designed to be shared. It is vital that people understand that true power does not appear sentient but is intellectually attainable. It is a powerful thing; to make this knowledge accessible. Simplifying greatness for others, helping them identify what follows a logical order and show that the steps to greatness are feasible. The work unavoidable. The skill set transferrable. What I am saying is a proxy that worked for me is not template to follow arbitrarily. I understand that many of the steps were exacted by many great people who were successful for different reasons. This suggested to me that the keys to manifesting greatness are inside of us. Then fundamentally we are the key to our own greatness. Waiting on some grand locksmith is time wasted because success is innate. It is inside of you. You must believe you are sufficient and that what you have is enough to just do it. Doing and failing makes you smarter than reading about it. For this narrative I use classmates who benefitted from the traditional educative model to compare and analyze in brief. I have graduated students from high school who in four years earned a bachelors and a masters comparable to the degrees I myself have earned. They have gone from former student to present competition simply by acquiring and applying readily available knowledge. I have students who had no interest in the traditional educative model but were able to achieve success through careful curation of their life goals. They were both able to experience their personal successes by coming up with a plan for success that fit their goals. Recognizing their resources to leap forward as mentioned was vital. Humility in recognizing what they knew, where they stood, what redirection they needed and then strategizing their development. This is what is meant by the importance of education. Being book and street smart. A student became the master, expediting the time by simply learning the industry they planned to enter. Just as another student had course work for the industry they planned to conquer. They were each successful in their own right. How cool is that? The lessons you receive, whether good or bad, provide a frame of reference. Developing systems to categorize the data as it is processed into useful information is the key to growth. This is the development of your frame of reference. Your frame of reference allows you to orient yourself. It is your life compass. Your frame of reference is your square. Get on it. When faced with difficulty, this frame of reference is what you will draw upon to find solutions. These are the tools on your utility belt. Your experiences, each milestone, your network, your resolve and your plan. Who can stop you now? The converse to this is destructive. The destructive mistakes serve to distract from your progress, subtract from your resources and to add unnecessary tracks to your course. The organization of thought allows for efficient processing. This bolsters your ability to choose wisely. Though there is no guarantee of success, you are able to determine your options. You are able make informed, logical assessments. You are afforded the opportunity to correlate effort versus gain, act versus consequence, as you are faced with difficulty. While developing your plan for success, milestones are necessary. These allow for tangible affirmations of your trajectory. This makes your goals feel real. The milestones serve to measure your steps and keep record of your time vested and resources acquired. Never confuse milestones with accomplishments. Never rest on your laurels. Allow for reflection. It allows for reflective processing. When reflecting, you retrace the steps given; adding to your plan for success. You provide personal quality control to improve best practices for yourself. You are to recognize your contributive efforts to your growth. It is accepting the responsibility and actualizing your efforts to improve for the next opportunity that will make you great. Time and tide wait for no man. The importance of conceptualizing time and mortality is vital. In this you develop a sense of urgency. Your must-have, got to get, I need, I want, by any means effort is manifested. This Intrinsic motivation is your ability to generate effort from within. It is your get-up-and-go. Your heart, will, and determination when no one pushes you. It allows you to take initiative. It takes pluck and a commitment to self to press on. Your passion is connected to your drive and motivations. Knowing what you want and seeing your work have its payoffs and costs. It is the key to giving maximum effort. That is why ideally you must identify your passions to ignite your drive. However, your drive cannot be fleeting. You cannot get bored. It cannot be a temporary interest when it comes to your plan for success. This plan is how you set up the rest of your life! It must survive all obstacles predicted and not. As you exact your plan for success, you will seek direction. You will need support. You may not receive the "YES" you expect. It is the ignorance of the word "NO" that will sustain you. This is perseverance. Everybody gets told no. So what? We only count yes's over here. The support not the supposed to is what matters. Absolutely. You are then approaching your greatness. You are now on your way.

"You gotta see what I've seen, look where I've looked
Touch what I've reached, and take what I've took
You gotta go where I've gone, walked where I've walked
To get where I'm at to speak what I've talked
You gotta lay where I've laid, stay where I've stayed
Play where I've played to make what I've made
You gotta move what I've moved, use what I used
Use tools how I use, use fools how I use…"
Beanie Sigel-The Truth

These conversations with my students, this accessibility was the idea for this book. I realized that for as different as my students were from each other they all had similar questions that begged an answer. My conversations with them were personal but the sentiment was the same for them all.

Everything you do or say is feedback for the audience. How you carry yourself is important. In my teacher role, I worked at schools with dress codes that were lax or the enforcement of those rules just did not happen. I would see kids sagging their pants, girls with head wraps. Now I get it, I went to high school as well. I did not want to wake up early and get dressed. I was getting good sleep. GREAT sleep. I hated the bus rides. I did not want to talk to anyone over eighteen either. I wore it on my face. It was a sea of us roaming the building anxious for dismissal. Hell, I worked with people who felt just like these students! The thing is this was feedback. This is feedback. As a teacher when I needed to hire young people, I would pass on those who left me with a sour taste until I spoke to them and got the truth about who they were, how smart they were, and what life meant to them. The circumstances called for these conversations. Like I said, I was their teacher. What if I was not? All that I saw would be all that I perceived. A sea filled with sagging pants and head wraps. What if I needed to hire them? What if I needed to hire you?

Maturity is in the details. The fine tooth combing over your plan is important. The elementary school of thought thinks life is a race. Think critically. Do not rush to decision. Take a moment to look at life in measured steps and you will then be able to create instances of success that will keep you. You build upon these small victories. They are the foundation of upward trajectory that shows you that you are heading in the right direction. Find your win. Create your winning season. Win your championship. Each win is a moment of validation. These moments are your pace. Pace is important. Delaying immediate reward, planning for a lifetime of it is maturity. Discipline is how you are going to arrive at your destination. Organize for success. Establishing your priorities brings structure to your life. What you prioritize determines where your energies are spent. It is simply what you value most and then carefully itemizing them. The sacrifices you may have to make short term will be forgotten when long term splendor arrives. Delaying immediate gratification for long term gains is the smartest play my friend. You have to think what is good for your lifetime not just the moment. The parties you will miss, the immediate fun, will not measure up to the lifelong rewards to be had. Your purpose will guide you and you will be changed by your experiences and your goals will to. All your efforts are driven by the quest for self-improvement. You modify your plan accordingly as you acquire and apply knowledge, but you never abandon your vision. Ever. You must see it through. You cannot stop. You owe it yourself to be the best you, you can offer the world.

Statements are not plans. Ideas are nothing without the determination to make them happen. Goals, actionable steps, milestones, and the agenda that develops are the plan. People have difficulty articulating a plan because they have not developed a personal construct to organize their thoughts to identify what they need and what actions are necessary as opposed to what they want. Identifying first ideally, what is most important to them and dedicating themselves to creating a life around that is the best way to govern yourself and establish your convictions. Your rules to live by. These cannot be compromised. You cannot allow them to be manipulated. This is your law. Regardless of environment or audience, your convictions are your truths. The key is not to let circumstances establish your moral compass or direct your behavior and focus. People look for patterns, they trust consistency. Circumstances change, integrity should not. Rain, sleet or snow, you should be consistent, the same ol' G.

Comfort is dangerous. Nothing great ever came from comfort. Nothing. For you to become who you plan to be, you have to grow. Without it, without growth you are dead. Facts. No dramatic pause and effect. In life. In the animal kingdom. In humanity. If you are not growing, you are dead and growth is not comfortable. Think about this. When you have growth spurts there is pain, clothes tighten, and shoes do not fit quite the same. There is discomfort in growth. This is transformation. In transformation there is the beauty of promise. Embrace it. If you are comfortable you are stagnant. You have found no reason to progress. There is nobility in work. There is pride in accomplishment. You cannot simply wait to feel like working. This is the mindset that leads to loss advantages. Loss of time, loss of capital, loss of opportunity. Embrace the difficulty. Challenge yourself. Discover the substance within you. Test your limits. It is a must that you raise your efforts to match your expectations. The converse is diminished. Why lower your performance to match menial expectations? It is insulting to self. As if. Setting the bar low is in fact evidence of fear.

Being too scared to try, too scared to confront your shortcomings. It is safe. There is no risk. However, you risk nothing by investing in yourself. You open yourself to possibilities that even if you do not obtain, you have learned from the efforts toward pursuing them. What do you have to lose by working toward your plan for success? What if your plan becomes reality? Get out of the bed. There is work to do.

Do not succumb to doubt. It is not real. It is counterproductive to your ascension. Doubt does little to grease the wheels of progress. It halts. It stagnates. Fear is nothing more than the projected culmination of insecurities that develop when the person focused on the loss instead of the lesson. Often this failure is not truly experienced by the people who are in fear. The expected feelings of uncertainty that occurs when you make efforts to grow and to build something new are just that: expected. This is not the same as doubt. The hesitancy is the search for sure footing for your decisions. Doubt is the lack of confidence in these decisions. This window of hesitancy is where doubt can set in. This is when the naysayers prey upon those unwilling to take a leap. The very reason limiting access to who you are is vital. People cast doubt. These people add no value while they steal belief and stifle your esteem. They have drunk the Kool-Aid. They have swallowed the red pill. They have readily accepted the fears of others. The fears of those who simply do nothing and are afraid to try. The excuse of fear is easier than the reason of effort.

No risk. No reward. What are you afraid of? It is not even real.

Do not see losing as failure. It is all part of the process of progression. It is necessary. It is valuable. You may face many challenges. Failure happens. Embrace it. They are opportunities to think critically. They are not to be considered defeats. They are necessary to your development. The lessons that are learned in failure are bountiful. The lessons gained in loss are just as valuable as those learned from winning. Do not see losing or failure. They are moments. They are not permanent. Progression is. The days go on. Time goes on. Whatever the present circumstances, accept them and work with it. Do no waste energy in regret and wishes for better days. Deal with what is in front of you. You must always be in pursuit of your grand self. In this life we are on journey toward our best version of ourselves. It is the effort you are willing to put toward your greatness, this self-investment, is how you will maximize your abilities. This maximization of your abilities increases your potential for success by making certain you are your supreme self. This is how you resolve situations and positively affect the best outcome for yourself when you have no one but yourself to rely on. Freedom from the fear of losing. This is independence.

Be present. That is, the current conversation, the present circumstance is what matters. Nothing more. It is the acquisition and application of knowledge that narrows the playing field regardless of industry. This bolsters your success margin. Be committed to the plan. You need the information from the resource. Period. Anything else is unnecessary. I had to learn how to effectively communicate. Thinking about the time I spent interacting, the many conversations with people. Thinking about how I engaged. I had to manage the situation, dictate the narrative. When I knew I would be in front of a resource or anybody with know-how, I had questions prepared. I took notes in my phone. I stored the number. I had an email pre drafted. I did not waste moments. I spoke with purpose and intent. I did not "um, you know what I mean" or mumble. The time of your stakeholders is valuable. I could not take for granted that I would get the opportunity to ask my questions again. You do not get time back. I began to value my time above all. That is what they mean when they say time is money. This is how you know how far you are willing to go, how committed you are and most importantly, what you are made of.

Do not waste time in pursuit of shortcuts. It takes the same amount of energy looking for a hand out as it does becoming the hand that feeds. Work while you work your network. If you are waiting to benefit from a hookup, you are at the mercy of that person. You are waiting for a savior. They rarely come. If you learn and acquire you make yourself valuable. If that person is no longer in a position to bestow those benefits, you still have made yourself harder to replace. They are your in. They are not the way to sustain. Be your own boss. Govern yourself. Lead yourself. You are born alone and you die alone. In the end all you have is yourself. All of this is to say, no one will have as much at stake in your outcome as you. You must actively pursue what is necessary in your pursuit of your best self. Do not leave it to chance. Do something that gets you closer to your dream every day. Every single day. Do not miss opportunities to learn and produce. Chase them. The reward will come. Doing the best you can each moment places you in the most advantageous situation for your next penultimate moment. Be open to perspective. Being rigid in your beliefs does not allow for growth. This rigidity creates a defensive mindset. Be biased to the outcome not the strategy. Use what works. Shed what does not. It is you clinging to thought at a personal level as opposed to functional. The information, thought, or process should be deemed valuable only if it is productive and progressive. It is not personal. It is true. The information does not have to be of popular opinion. It does have to be factual. Beware of people who want to be right for the sake of being right arbitrarily. Holding on to thought just because is detrimental to your growth. It indicates limited thought. You want to acquire perspective and apply thought. It will sharpen you as you move forward over time. Fear of failure, mistakes or rejection should not be the reason you do nothing. Perfection is not necessary for success.

There will be moments of depletion. There will also be moments of restoration. Life is cyclical that way. Wait on them. They will be enough of each. This breaks up monotony. The peaks and valleys is where life is lived. Do not die waiting. Pace and patience are moments of movement not standstill. These are different stages of progress; not stagnation. It is knowing how to use time effectively that will dictate how useful you can become. Being useful is not the same as being used. It is purposeful. It leads to value adding decisions governing the direction of your life. Your actions should add value. You are worth it. Staying inspired makes every other success possible, greatness is accessible.

Friendship is easy even when conversations are difficult. Friendship should not be forced and they come at zero cost to who you are. Be leery of people who want to be along for the ride as opposed to figuring out how to make a way. Similar character values are more important than similar interests. What a person expects of themselves they typically expect of others. Pay attention to what people want for themselves. If it is not much, there is no resource there. You cannot let people make you accept their version of reality. That is not your suit. One of my best friends in the world loves me enough to look me in the eyes and say without hesitancy, "That is stupid." They do and did not join me in my aimless pursuits. They pointed it out and disengaged. They would not participate in my peril, they would only be available for my ascension.

Happiness is a destination. Take residence. Fun is just a visit. Fun people visit too in the guise as friends and family at times. Happy-like distractions take you away from the work necessary to achieve true happiness. These distractions can provide a comfortable level of complacency that the time lost to partying, boozing, drug abuse or laziness is wasted and progress stalled. They are exactly that, distractions. They do not advance the agenda. They in fact take away resources that could be used for self-investment. The greatness that is ahead is not given but is available. The accessibility of the resources is not infinite and depends on when you take advantage of them. This can create inequity as you pursue your endeavors. It is because of this inequity the disparity between achievements has peaks and valleys; that is, the different levels may make the feasibility of the success plan feel impossible as it appears your counterparts achieve more. This again is the fallacy of that false comparison.

It is nice to be important. It is more important to be nice. Be nice. Practice it. Be patient in the face of confrontation. Even in the face of an asshole. Always be nice. It is the greatest camouflage. EVER. I know what you are thinking, it is hard, and it is ridiculously trying. It may not make sense in the moment, but being nice is powerful. It is your absolute control of your emotions. It is being present and cognizant of what is happening around you, everything that is going on, who is in your space and what lead to any point of duress. It diffuses people and situations by helping you manage personalities. It gives the impression that you are in control of the situation. When you initiate nicely, you level the playing field of communication. It affords you the advantage of seeing the response of the people you engage with. Their temperament, their humor, and ultimately their logic is revealed in these exchanges. The importance of using decorum as a weapon is undervalued. Do not tip your hand. Play your ace last. I learned this the hard way. I would be short with coworkers. I would be visibly displeased with superiors. I would go in on group members who did not pull their weight in projects. People knew I was competent, but they did not want to work with me. I got passed over for leadership positions regularly. It was not until I had a private conversation with a respected mentor who simply informed me in short: people did not like me. They did not want to work for me. I had a reputation as abrasive. I had yet to learn how to endear myself to my audience. It was all unintentional. I did not realize that I was a walking brand. They thought I was the angry black guy and the one man in America with resting "I wish a fool would." face. I paid no attention to how I was perceived. I foolishly thought my work spoke for itself. Merit and intellect though respected are not principle reason for selection. You can alienate yourself. You might be the best dressed, prettiest thing, or the smartest person in the room but if the audience does not like you, you will not prosper. People should root for you. Give them a reason to. Everything you do is feedback for people observing you. How you conduct yourself is your brand. The impressions you leave people with, the attitudes that evoke emotions out of your audience. These emotions are what people attribute to you and the more positive engagements you have with people you leave a trail of people who will champion your efforts and applaud your presence to others. How you carry yourself, your attention to detail about yourself is feedback for the audience. If you are not patient enough for your own success, why should anyone give you the responsibility to govern theirs?

Your reputation is everything. We are not talking street cred here people. We are not talking falsified grandiose stories of events that simply did not happen but make great songs and episodes of Power. It is your brand. It speaks for you. It should be honest. Spend time cultivating you as opposed to wasting time maintaining a lie. This honesty will allow you to be comfortable in any setting. Your reputation is tied to how you make people feel about your presence. Do you increase value? Do you leave people with good vibes? Are you reliable? A reputation is designed by committee. You define it, but the way it develops depends on the perceptions of others. Your reputation lives a very real existence. It has a life of its own. It represents the collective mental construct everyone you have ever engaged with has about-you. Your reputation arrives before you do. It is a hypothesis of who you are based partially on your own actions and interactions with others but also on the perception others have about others' perceptions of you (I know, right?). It can open a door for you or shut it before you even realize there was a door to knock on at all. You can positively influence your reputation but never control it. This is the case with all things external to us, but your reputation remains one of our most prized resources. A reputation represents the way others look at us. Ironically, it is simultaneously critically important and utterly trivial. Utterly trivial because if we have a healthy self-perception, self-esteem and are self-aware you do not need others to think well of you to reconcile decisions you have made for yourself. Many find difficulty, with this and find their sense of value vulnerable to the opinions of others. You cannot let the opinions of others decide your life. It is important to have a healthy relationship with you. Love you. This is critically important, because even those of us with the most resilient self-esteem live in a world connected to others and need a good reputation for practical purposes. It is hard to have friends if people think you are mean-spirited and hard to make a living in any capacity if people think you're lazy, unreliable, or dishonest. Our reputation is a tool for creating or maintaining our self-esteem but it is centrally a tool for practical navigation through daily life. It is fragile. Building a good reputation requires effort, patience, and time. Destroying a good reputation only requires a single moment. One misstep. One mistake. The secret to building a good reputation is being honest with who you are. Be a person who deserves the salutations and praise. Take consistent action that embodies the characteristics you want others to associate with you. Let your actions speak for you. Your reputation is the reason people are willing to stake their reputations, vouching for the experience of your actions. This is how you acquire people equity. Your reach is furthered as your network increases. So does the quality of the opportunities. Leaving people with the "warm and fuzzies" while being of service is valuable position. You add value to the life of the people you engage with and they remember this. They appreciate the quality experiences, the laughs, the salutations and the situational solvency. This is the power of being useful. This is the importance of being nice. This is not saying allow yourself to be punked or subjected to abuse by being arbitrarily and overly agreeable at your own expense. That is absolutely not what I am saying. Do not be used. Be a resource. It has value. Know your limits. Know your NO. You should advocate for yourself always. You should be your biggest fan. Rooting for yourself. Humility is how you receive your blessings. Success, no matter how large, has a small beginning. An idea, stretched by effort, forged by passion. Difficult pathways hide your hidden manna. There is nobility in the work. The easier the path the smaller the reward and applause for your accomplishment. You do not get credit for the hills you skip up. Only the mountains you climb. This perseverance through difficulty is commitment. Remaining resolute in your commitment is how you develop character, this is how you find your moral depth and your conviction. From out of the mud and concrete a rose blooms with stems stronger than those who grew up through the calm on easy street. Be current in world events. Knowing the latest fashions, dances and what happened on what show is cool and all, but what is going on in the world that you live? You might be getting left behind and not even know it. This is survival. You might be clinging to an antiquated way of thinking. You might be bobbing when it is time to weave. Be an active learner. Learning has to become habitual and ritualistic. You have to embrace the constant development. Organizing how you think, thinking about how you process the information you are given is important. Ask yourself, do you know what you know? Do you even know how smart you are? Taking inventory of what you know and need to know is instrumental to creating your plan for success

A reputation is delicate. It requires continuous curating. Regularity is crucial. If you live up to your reputation 99% of the time but fail to do so 1% of the time, you risk irrevocable damage. What if the person you let down is highly influential in your network? A good reputation should not be the end game in itself, but rather a natural outgrowth of your striving to be the person you most want to be. This personal honesty and accountability crafts your reputation. To ignore the practical importance of a good reputation cheats you of many opportunities you might otherwise enjoy. Caring about our reputation does not mean we need others to like us. You are not desperate nor lame. It means recognizing the usefulness of public perception to advance your agenda. No hidden formula. But you must remain true to yourself. Your true spectacular self. Fitting in is the worst. Finding your fit is the best. People are dying to be regular. Stifling themselves to fit other people's perceptions of who they are and for what? To appease people who do not see the greatness in themselves? Tuh.

Do not get your life and life confused. The intersection of life and your life is very real but rarely understood. Accept that these are two different things. There is life, incessant and impersonal. It goes on. With or without you. It goes on. It is the collection of circumstances compounded with time. It has no personal stake in your outcome. It is unforgiving. Your life is the opposite of this. It is finite. It is personal. You can forgive yourself. Recognizing the mutual exclusivity of both and the symbiotic nature of their intersection helps you not take things personal. For example, you and some jerk both arrive at a red light. He is in a rush. You are not. He honks his horn aggressively. When the light turns green because he feels you did not take off fast enough. He gives you the finger. Meanwhile you were sitting coolly, listening to your favorite song with your seat belt completely oblivious to what just happened. Life is the red light. The circumstances that brought each of you to that light is a manifestation of all of each of your decisions and efforts to live as life unfolds. That moment for each of you is your individual lives. It is not the light he should be mad at nor anyone else in traffic. He should be accountable for what made him late in the first place. In that moment you could become aggravated and give them the finger, you can allow it to affect your day. When you pause and think about the situation in the context of life and your life, it lets you reconcile the ordeal and move past it. Why even bother to engage? Value these moments of clarity. They are peace. My father would always end our conversations with an "I love you," followed by "Do not argue with strangers." It was a simple enough piece of advice that I would gloss over. I asked him to elaborate on one of the many Sundays we would have breakfast and I would catch him up with what was going on with my very own plan for success. We discussed how we see people at a surface level. Age, dress or costume, race or color, gender etc. He would point out how these were simple markers that people lazily used to form conclusions about the people they encounter. Simple but they do not get give the depth to the life story of any individual. We cannot see the perils people suffer through daily. You cannot see the stresses that sour the dispositions on the faces you pass by on the street. You were not present for the scars, the wrinkles, the bruises or scrapes. The daily abuses. You do not see the story of the person just the book cover. You only see the surface. Do not penalize them for their outbursts, their angered faces, their middle fingers. You have not read their pages to form a conclusion. Do not argue with strangers.

Greatness is tailored to the individual. The way your greatness manifests is where we differentiate. Where we find similarity is in the work necessary to achieve. What you wish to be great at is your choice, however the work, the effort, the study, the sacrifice will await you just as it awaits anyone. This offering of yourself is not to be wasted as you pursue the greatest you. Whatever you want to be great at requires work. It is unavoidable. Stop trying for shortcuts. We may have strengths in different areas but our goal is to optimize our chances and strive for greatness. I may have the best bars and you may be an amazing vocalist but in our respective greatness, we both worked voraciously to make a hit song. We all have our greatness. Simple. You see society embraces the bell curve. Globally they tell you to fit in and comply. Blend in and be average. Do not rock the boat. Do not make waves. Be a little bit, but not too little. BE present but do not distract. That will be just right. For whom? What if I crave more? What if I want it all? What if I want something different? People will try to convince you that you, YOU, yourself are regular. They will come in droves. Sometimes disguised as family and friends. They will tell you that your dreams are too big and that, you are not being realistic. Fuck these people, with a smile. Commit to your success. They were defeated by their effort. They lost to their doubt. They did not embrace the work. They settled and their perspective is skewed. They accepted circumstances that very well were beyond their control as the limit to their ascension. People soured them on other people as well. They did not network. They cliqued. They group thought. Gather your own data. Make your own conclusion. You have to see for yourself. They will not see your vision. They do not have the sight you see. It is not easy to commit to the labor of loving yourself enough. Loving yourself despite all the self-inflicted reasons and false justifications of how you should not. Loving yourself enough to face your shortcomings and make them strengths. This is not easy. In this, doing the difficult things only serves one purpose. Letting you know what limitations you need to break through. Embracing the work necessary to break through. The challenges that will awaken your inner greatness will be incessant. Your greatness is outside of your comfort zone. Challenge yourself continuously to learn more. To be more. Consistency will lead to your greater self. You have to realize that all your efforts, all your struggles are purposeful. Climb that mountain. The climb. It is a lifestyle. It has to become habit. Second nature. Consistency is permanence.

The importance of appreciation cannot be overlooked. It is key to reflection. When you appreciate, you attribute value to that person, that item and those experiences. You recognize the benefit they contributed to your ascension. This is how you prepare for your abundance. How are you supposed to be endowed with more, when you currently have everything that you need at this very moment and have not bothered to use it? You have not shown appreciation by recognizing what you have and where you are. If you are committed to make excuses as to why what you have is not sufficient to be greater, you have already lost. You can complain and make excuses and find others who validate this mentality. You can find others in the same place of inactivity and they will try to convince you that "it is ok to stay this way…" I am here to tell you that if you want better start where you are, use the resources you already have. In this day and age a good portion of your resources are at your fingertips. Do not wait for the right moment, because there is no right moment. The time is now. The timing of which you can effect by exacting your resources strategically to positively influence your learning curve. Understanding the sense of urgency and timing allows you to appropriately use this most cherished resource. Nothing is a waste of time if you gain knowledge and use the experience to gain wisdom. Remember you are readying yourself and approaching your success. Find the small victories daily to keep pressing forward. This is the simplicity of greatness.

"Listen to different scriptures, they teach on God
And if you ain't never met him, don't speak on God
I'm serious about religion, this shit's ain't no song
I'm hearing niggas makin' up scriptures, and playing along
Probably saying I'm the hypocrite, for judging these folks
But you can tell he ain't a Christian, by the way that he spoke
I pray for everybody, hoping that they hear that voice
The one that paralyzes you from head down, boy
When you're aware of your surroundings, yet you still can't move
Water shooting outta your eyes you hear this dude
And the voice is much louder, than the voice that you
Thought was the voice of the holy spirit
Gon' change your life when you hear it
And the next morn', you wake up and the world look lighter
The grass greener, and the sun brighter
I know the feeling first hand, I witnessed the sights
When I allowed the Lord to come in my life
And it was like (heaven, heaven...)
But I'm a man, I ain't perfect
That's a poor excuse, that ain't working
I asked him for forgiveness, for every sin I commit
Hopefully he gonna let me stay on his list"
Scarface -Heaven

Thank you for your time.

Akwaaba!* Allow me to introduce myself. My name is Samuel Agyarko Jr. founder of the A-Team Educational Consulting with RTI! This open letter allows me to share my experiences, my life's work and what defines my voice. I am a spiritually driven child of Ghanaian immigrants. Myself being a successful product of Chicago's inner city and Public Schools system began teaching in the urban community, I recognized the deficit in leadership that many students faced. I was compelled to act.

In pursuing higher education, I earned my Bachelor of Science in Applied Computer Science, with a minor in Economics, and I am Illinois State Board Certified in Business, Computer Science and Technology. As a lover of knowledge I pursued my Masters in Educational Leadership to further my understanding of what is necessary to be an academic leader. I have 13 years of teaching experience at the elementary and secondary level in the Jeffrey Manor, Englewood & South Holland communities of Illinois, respectively.

As a product of the Hip Hop generation, I understand the importance of culturally responsive efforts to engage students. I accepted the charge to expedite the development of young men and young women. It is my hope to create thought provoking, conscious conversation for the masses by building leaders.

CPSIA information can be obtained
at www.ICGtesting.com
Printed in the USA
BVHW041726250820
587281BV00007B/273

9 781985 735989